Cyber Security Cyber Resilience

I0009745

About the Author

With a distinguished military career in Communications and IT, the author brings unparalleled expertise and perspective to the field of cybersecurity. Over two decades of immersive experience in digital security have shaped their comprehensive understanding of the intricacies involved in cybersecurity today. This book, Cyber Security Cyber Resilience, reflects their commitment to illuminating the critical challenges faced by organizations as they navigate the landscape of evolving digital threats.

During their extensive career, which spans over 20 years, the author has successfully developed and implemented robust cybersecurity controls that protect various organizations from a wide range of threats. They have collaborated closely with local and central government departments in the UK, enhancing their ability to tackle complex security challenges. Their military background instills a disciplined approach to problem-solving and operational excellence, which is evident in their strategic perspective on cybersecurity measures.

Academically, the author has invested in a robust education that supports their professional endeavors. With a strong foundational knowledge in IT and communications, they have not only excelled in practical applications but also developed a passion for sharing knowledge with others. Their journey as a writer began as a way to bridge the gap between technical complexities and real-world applications, aiming to make cybersecurity accessible and engaging for a broad audience.

Personal experiences serve as a backdrop to their writing style, which is characterized by clarity, relatability, and a hands-on approach. The author's passion for teaching and sharing knowledge shines through their work, as they strive to demystify the complexities of cybersecurity. Recognizing the importance of keeping content engaging, they infuse their writing with real-world experiences, aiming to empower readers to take actionable steps toward enhancing their cybersecurity resilience.

Driven by a mission to illuminate the importance of cybersecurity in an increasingly digital world, the author seeks to inspire organizations and individuals alike to embrace proactive measures. With goals of further contributing to the field through consulting, speaking engagements, and future publications, they are committed to fostering a culture of cybersecurity awareness and resilience. Through Cyber Security Cyber Resilience, they invite readers to join them on this journey toward a safer digital landscape.

Table of Contents

Chapter 1: Introduction to Cyber Resilience

Chapter 2: Understanding Cyber Threat Landscape

Chapter 3: Fundamentals of Supplier Assurance

Chapter 4: Defense in Depth Strategy

Chapter 5: Risk Management in Cyber Security

Chapter 6: Incident Response Planning

Chapter 7: Integrating Security Across the Network

Chapter 8: Building a Cyber Resilient Culture

(1) - 8.1 Employee Training and Awareness Programs

(2) - 8.2 Encouraging Reporting and Transparency

(3) - 8.3 Leadership and Governance in Cyber Resilience

Chapter 9: Developing Cyber Resilience Metrics

(1) - 9.1 Key Performance Indicators for Cyber Resilience

(2) - 9.2 Monitoring and Evaluating Metrics

(3) - 9.3 Reporting and Communicating Metrics to Stakeholders

Chapter 10: Technology Solutions for Cyber Resilience

Chapter 11: Compliance and Regulatory Considerations

Chapter 12: Business Continuity and Cyber Resilience

Chapter 13: Third-Party Risk Management

Chapter 14: Cyber Resilience Frameworks and Standards

Chapter 15: Future Directions in Cyber Resilience

(1) - 15.1 Evolving Cyber Threats and Resilience Tactics

(2) - 15.2 Role of Collaboration in Enhancing Resilience

(3) - 15.3 Anticipating Future Regulatory Changes

Chapter 1: Introduction to Cyber Resilience

1.1 Defining Cyber Resilience

Cyber resilience represents a crucial evolution in how we approach security, moving far beyond traditional metrics that solely focus on preventing breaches. While most security measures aim to block threats, cyber resilience emphasizes maintaining operational continuity, even when cyber incidents occur. This shift in perspective recognizes that no system is completely invulnerable. Therefore, organizations must prepare for potential disruptions by implementing strategies that allow them to recover and continue operations despite adverse events. This proactive mindset entails being ready to face cyber threats, minimizing their impact, and ensuring that business processes can quickly resume following an incident. Cyber resilience requires a cohesive strategy that links incident response capabilities with business continuity planning, allowing organizations to react swiftly and effectively when an attack occurs.

To effectively build a resilient cyber infrastructure, organizations must consider the integration of three key components: people, processes, and technologies. The workforce plays a pivotal role, as human behavior often influences security outcomes. Training and awareness initiatives are essential in equipping employees to recognize threats and respond appropriately. Processes must be thoroughly documented and regularly tested to ensure that everyone understands their roles in the event of a cyber incident. Technologies must work in concert to provide real-time monitoring and responses to threats, ensuring that systems are capable of adapting as new vulnerabilities emerge. By harmoniously blending these elements, businesses can create an agile and robust cyber ecosystem that not only protects against threats but empowers the workforce to engage meaningfully in safeguarding critical assets.

As organizations embark on their journey toward cyber resilience, a valuable practice is to continuously assess and refine their strategies. Regularly revisiting security policies and training protocols can uncover areas for improvement, promoting an adaptive culture that prioritizes resilience. This approach not only fortifies defenses but also enhances overall cybersecurity posture, aligning organizational goals with an ever-evolving landscape of threats. Prioritizing resilience in cyber initiatives ensures preparedness, reduces downtime, and fosters confidence in the organization's ability to face future challenges.

1.2 Importance of Cyber Resilience in Modern Networks

The increasing complexity of modern networks necessitates a robust cyber resilience strategy that can withstand a range of potential disruptions. As organizations integrate more devices, cloud services, and interconnected systems, the attack surface they present to potential threats expands exponentially. This intricate web of connections makes it imperative for organizations to adopt a proactive approach toward resilience. Cyber resilience goes beyond traditional security measures, focusing not only on preventing breaches but also on maintaining operational continuity in the event of an incident. By fostering resilience, businesses can quickly adapt and recover from disruptions, whether they stem from cyberattacks, system failures, or human error.

Analyzing case studies highlights how effective cyber resilience strategies have significantly enhanced organizational survival amidst adversity. For instance, consider a well-known breach within a major retailer that compromised millions of customer records. The company, having pre-established a comprehensive incident response plan and resilient infrastructure, managed to contain the breach swiftly. They not only minimized the financial repercussions but also reinforced customer trust through transparent communication and timely remediation steps. Another case involved a healthcare provider that suffered a ransomware attack. Their investment in cyber resilience paid off as they were able to restore systems and access to critical patient data within hours, ensuring uninterrupted care during a crisis. These examples illustrate that organizations with well-integrated cyber resilience practices are better positioned to navigate challenges, emerging stronger in competitive landscapes.

To enhance cyber resilience, professionals in the field should prioritize integrating supplier assurance and defense in depth into their strategies. This means assessing the security posture of third-party vendors and incorporating multi-layered defenses that can mitigate risks across various points in the network. By continuously evaluating and evolving their defenses, organizations can cultivate a culture of preparedness and adaptability, which is essential in today's dynamic threat environment. A practical tip for cybersecurity professionals is to conduct regular resilience drills that simulate potential attacks or failures, fostering a hands-on understanding of response procedures and identifying any gaps in their strategies.

1.3 Key Concepts and Terminology

Cyber resilience encompasses a variety of essential terms and concepts that help establish a common framework for understanding how organizations can withstand, adapt to, and recover from cyber incidents. It is often defined as the ability to prepare for, respond to, and recover from cyber security threats while maintaining essential functions. Resilience is not solely about protecting data and networks; it also involves ensuring that an organization can continue its operations despite adverse cyber events. It incorporates risk management, incident response, and recovery strategies within its paradigm. This holistic view recognizes that threats are not just technical issues but also involve human and organizational components that need addressing. Key terminology associated with cyber resilience includes risk tolerance, which refers to the level of risk an organization is willing to accept, and business continuity planning, an approach used to ensure operations continue smoothly during and after a cyber incident. Such definitions create a shared understanding, enabling professionals to discuss strategies effectively and develop comprehensive resilience programs.

The relationship between cyber resilience and traditional cybersecurity approaches is one that emphasizes their complementary roles. Traditional cybersecurity focuses predominantly on the protection of devices, networks, and data from potential breaches and attacks. It involves deploying security tools such as firewalls, intrusion detection systems, and anti-malware solutions to create a protective barrier around an organization's digital assets. However, this approach alone is insufficient in today's threat landscape, where attacks can happen despite robust defense measures. Cyber resilience expands this perspective by incorporating proactive measures that consider the likelihood of an attack succeeding. It emphasizes preparedness, detection, and recovery, effectively bridging the gap between prevention and response. By adopting a cyber resilience framework, organizations can not only fortify their defenses but also cultivate an agile response capability, allowing them to bounce back quickly from disruptions. This approach aligns with the concept of Defense in Depth, where layers of security are complemented by strategies for resilience, ensuring a comprehensive shield against a multitude of cyber threats.

As cyber threats and attacks evolve, organizations need to think beyond just preventative measures. One practical tip for enhancing cyber resilience is to integrate incident response exercises into regular business operations. Conducting tabletop exercises not only prepares teams for real-world scenarios but also uncovers gaps in processes and technology that could impair recovery efforts. Engaging in these training sessions promotes a culture of resilience among employees, fostering a shared understanding of their roles and responsibilities during a cyber incident. This proactive approach ensures that when a cyber event does occur, the organization is better positioned to respond effectively and minimize downtime.

Chapter 2: Understanding Cyber Threat Landscape

2.1 Types of Cyber Threats

Cyber threats can be broadly categorized into several types, each posing unique risks to organizations. Malware is one of the most prevalent forms, encompassing a range of malicious software designed to infiltrate and damage systems. This can include viruses, worms, ransomware, and spyware, which can lead to significant data loss, financial damage, or unauthorized access to sensitive information. Phishing attacks are another major threat, involving deceptive communications that trick individuals into revealing personal information, such as passwords or bank details. Cybercriminals often use these tactics to impersonate trusted entities, making it essential for professionals to recognize warning signs, such as suspicious links or unfamiliar sender addresses. Insider threats, which originate from within an organization, often stem from employees or contractors who misuse their access to compromise data or systems. This type of threat can be particularly challenging to identify, as it may involve legitimate users acting maliciously or simply making careless mistakes.

Real-world examples underscore the frequency and impact of these threats on organizational security. The 2017 WannaCry ransomware attack, which affected hundreds of thousands of computers across 150 countries, illustrates the devastating potential of malware. This incident encrypted user files and held them hostage, crippling many businesses and hospitals that relied on their systems for operations. Phishing is exemplified by the 2020 Twitter hack, where attackers gained access to high-profile accounts by deceiving employees into disclosing their credentials through well-crafted phishing messages. Such incidents reveal that even large organizations can fall victim to social engineering tactics. Insider threats are highlighted by the case of Edward Snowden, who leaked classified data from the National Security Agency, leading to significant breaches of trust and security. These examples not only illustrate the diverse nature of cyber threats but also highlight the critical need for organizations to foster a culture of vigilance and implement robust defenses.

To enhance resilience, professionals must prioritize continuous education and training for employees at all levels. Regular drills that simulate cyberattack scenarios can improve recognition and response capabilities. It's also vital to maintain up-to-date security protocols and employ multi-layered defense strategies that account for various types of threats, including implementing advanced detection software and conducting thorough audits of user activity. By understanding the landscape of cyber threats and actively engaging in preventive measures, organizations can significantly reduce risk and protect their critical assets.

2.2 Emerging Threats and Trends

Recent developments in cyber threats have shifted the landscape starkly, particularly with the rise of ransomware-as-a-service (RaaS) and targeted supply chain attacks. RaaS has democratized access to sophisticated ransomware tools, allowing even those with minimal technical expertise to launch devastating attacks. Cybercriminals provide a subscription-based model where users can rent ransomware kits to facilitate their malicious objectives. This accessibility has led to an increase in attacks on organizations of all sizes, often crippling operations and demanding hefty ransoms for data recovery. In parallel, supply chain attacks have emerged as a critical concern as they exploit trust relationships between organizations and their vendors. By infiltrating less secure vendors, threat actors can gain entry into larger, more secure organizations, multiplying the impact and scope of their attacks. Notable examples, such as the SolarWinds breach, highlight how vulnerabilities can cascade through interconnected systems, affecting thousands of entities and exposing sensitive data on a massive scale.

To tackle these evolving threats, predictive analysis techniques are becoming increasingly essential for anticipating emerging trends in the cyber threat landscape. By leveraging data analytics, organizations can identify patterns and behaviors indicative of potential attacks, allowing them to proactively strengthen their defenses. Techniques such as machine learning and artificial intelligence can analyze vast amounts of data from various sources, including threat intelligence feeds, network traffic, and past incident reports. These analyses can discover anomalies and predict future threats before they materialize into actual attacks. Additionally, incorporating threat modeling and simulations can provide insights into possible attack vectors, enhancing an organization's preparedness. Organizations that integrate these predictive techniques into their security frameworks can better allocate resources, prioritize risk management strategies, and design resilient systems that not only defend against current threats but also adapt to unforeseen challenges.

Staying ahead in the rapidly changing cybersecurity environment requires a commitment to continuous learning and adaptation. Cybersecurity professionals should engage in regular threat intelligence sharing and collaboration with peers and industry groups. This collaborative approach not only improves individual organizational defenses but also strengthens the broader cyber ecosystem, making it more difficult for threat actors to exploit vulnerabilities.

2.3 Assessing Threat Severity and Impact

Risk assessment models are essential tools in identifying and prioritizing threats that can impact an organization's cybersecurity posture. These models allow cybersecurity professionals to evaluate the potential impact of threats based on their likelihood and the severity of their consequences. For instance, frameworks such as the NIST Cyber Security Framework and FAIR (Factor Analysis of Information Risk) provide structured methodologies to quantify risk, combining both qualitative and quantitative measures. By employing these frameworks, consultants and architects can systematically determine which threats pose the greatest danger, enabling them to allocate resources and implement controls effectively. The right model helps organizations to focus on high-priority threats that could lead to significant data breaches or service disruptions, thereby enhancing overall resilience.

Effectively communicating the severity of identified threats to stakeholders is just as crucial as assessing them. A well-organized reporting framework serves to bridge the gap between technical findings and business decision-making. Utilizing visual aids such as heat maps or risk matrices can convey complex information in a straightforward manner, allowing stakeholders from non-technical backgrounds to grasp the implications of risks quickly. Furthermore, maintaining transparent communication ensures stakeholders understand not only the risk but also the rationale behind recommended security measures. Cybersecurity professionals should tailor their messages to address the specific concerns and priorities of their audience, thereby fostering a culture of proactive risk management within the organization.

Incorporating regular assessments and updates to threat severity evaluations can significantly contribute to an organization's preparedness against cyber threats. As the cyber landscape evolves, so too do the threats posed by adversaries; therefore, continuous monitoring and reassessment are vital. A practical tip is to establish a routine review process that aligns with incident response and business continuity planning efforts. This ensures that as new threats emerge, organizations can adapt their strategies promptly, maintaining resilience and protecting critical assets with agility and foresight.

Chapter 3: Fundamentals of Supplier Assurance

3.1 Overview of Supplier Assurance Frameworks

Various frameworks and standards play a crucial role in guiding supplier security assessment and assurance practices. Commonly adopted frameworks such as ISO 27001, NIST SP 800-171, and the Cybersecurity Framework (CSF) from NIST provide structured approaches for managing risks associated with suppliers. These frameworks emphasize the importance of assessing cybersecurity controls and require organizations to evaluate their suppliers' compliance with recognized standards. Aligning with these frameworks helps organizations establish a consistent method to measure supplier risk, ensuring that suppliers adhere to indispensable cybersecurity protocols that protect sensitive data throughout the supply chain. Furthermore, sector-specific models such as the Payment Card Industry Data Security Standard (PCI DSS) are vital for organizations within financial and payment sectors, providing detailed requirements for safeguarding customer payment information during processing and storage.

Incorporating supplier assurance in an organization's overall risk management strategy is vital to achieving comprehensive risk mitigation. When organizations treat supplier security as a core component of their risk management, they create a resilient network capable of withstanding potential supply chain threats. The interconnectedness of modern business means that suppliers often hold critical access to sensitive data and systems, making their security posture essential to the primary organization's resilience. A robust supplier assurance strategy fosters transparency and trust, enhancing collaboration and reducing the potential impact of third-party vulnerabilities. By proactively identifying and addressing potential risks associated with suppliers, entities can not only protect themselves but also ensure compliance with regulatory requirements and industry standards, positioning themselves favorably in the market.

Establishing a systematic approach to supplier assessment and assurance is not merely a best practice; it is a necessity in an era where cyber threats evolve rapidly. Organizations should regularly revisit and refine their assessment processes, leveraging insights gained from previous audits and evaluations to bolster their defense strategies effectively. Engaging with suppliers openly about security policies encourages an atmosphere of accountability and contributes to overall organizational resilience.

3.2 Evaluating Supplier Security Postures

Evaluating and assessing supplier security measures is a critical step to ensure that they align with your internal security policies. Start by examining the supplier's security documentation, such as their security policies, compliance certifications, and incident response plans. Look for adherence to recognized standards like ISO 27001 or NIST Cybersecurity Framework, as these benchmarks provide a solid foundation for evaluating security procedures. Engaging in direct conversations with suppliers about their measures can also offer valuable insights. Inquire about their approach to data protection, network security, and employee training. Understanding their risk management practices, including how they identify and mitigate potential threats, is essential. Compatibility with your own security framework not only minimizes risks but also fosters a collaborative security culture. By employing a comprehensive assessment strategy that includes questionnaires and third-party evaluations, organizations can determine the robustness of a supplier's security measures and make informed decisions about partnership durability.

Audits and risk assessments play a pivotal role in continuously monitoring the security postures of suppliers. Conducting regular audits allows organizations to ensure their suppliers maintain compliance with agreed-upon security standards and protocols. These audits can include on-site assessments, document reviews, and interviews with key personnel. It's essential to incorporate a standardized audit schedule to maintain objectivity and transparency in the evaluation process. Complementing these audits with periodic risk assessments can provide deeper insights into potential vulnerabilities. This involves evaluating how changes in the supplier's business model, technology stack, or threat landscape may impact their security readiness. Leveraging tools and methodologies such as threat modeling and penetration testing enables organizations to identify any weaknesses and remediate them proactively. Keeping a continuous dialogue with suppliers about findings and recommended improvements facilitates a strong partnership and enhances overall security resilience.

Implementing a strategy where both parties engage in regular communication about security incidents or near misses creates an environment of transparency and mutual interest in security goals. Consider establishing a shared platform for reporting and managing security-related issues, as this can streamline responses and corrective actions. Furthermore, employing metrics and reporting frameworks can help quantify a supplier's security performance over time, making it easier to identify trends and areas for improvement. Regular engagement, combined with a structured monitoring process, not only strengthens the supplier relationship but also builds a more resilient security posture across the network.

3.3 Establishing Trust with Suppliers

Building and maintaining trust-based relationships with suppliers is essential for organizations aiming to enhance their cybersecurity posture. It starts with the establishment of consistent practices across all organizational levels. The approach should be systematic, fostering a culture where collaboration and shared goals are prioritized. Organizations should engage in regular assessments of supplier performance, not just through audits but by integrating suppliers into ongoing discussions about risk management. Including suppliers in strategy meetings and decision-making processes can significantly bolster trust, as it shows that their input is valued and that they are considered partners in the organization's security landscape. Ensuring that suppliers have clear expectations and understand the organization's cybersecurity framework will fortify this trust, as transparency in requirements leads to more effective collaborations.

Effective communication is pivotal in nurturing a trusting relationship with suppliers. Open lines of dialogue encourage transparency, which is vital for fostering a collaborative approach to security. Organizations should establish regular communication channels, allowing for prompt discussions on potential threats or vulnerabilities that may arise in the vendor's domain. This two-way communication not only helps maintain a shared understanding of security protocols but also creates an environment where both parties feel comfortable sharing concerns and insights. Moreover, sharing relevant data and forecasts helps suppliers calibrate their security measures in alignment with the organization's evolving threats. By enhancing transparency through effective communication, organizations can both elevate the security posture of their supply chain and reinforce trust with their suppliers, creating a resilient network that can withstand emerging cybersecurity challenges.

To solidify trust, it is paramount to recognize that building relationships with suppliers is an ongoing journey rather than a one-time effort. Practicing regular feedback sessions can help in addressing any issues early on and adjusting strategies as needed. Developing mutual training sessions can also enhance understanding of cybersecurity standards and practices. Furthermore, organizations should also consider offering incentives for suppliers who demonstrate a commitment to cybersecurity objectives. This reinforcement not only cultivates loyalty but also encourages suppliers to invest in their own security frameworks, ultimately benefiting the broader network. By committing to these practices, organizations can not only achieve trust with their suppliers but also create a robust line of defense that contributes significantly to overall operational resilience.

Chapter 4: Defense in Depth Strategy

4.1 Principles of Defense in Depth

Defense in depth is a fundamental strategy in cybersecurity that emphasizes the importance of layering multiple security controls to protect an organization's sensitive information and assets. At its core, this approach recognizes that no single security measure is foolproof. Instead, it advocates for a comprehensive security posture that engages several distinct layers of defense, such as physical security, network security, application security, and data protection. This multifaceted strategy not only aids in minimizing the impact of a potential security breach but also enhances the overall resilience of the organization. By distributing security controls throughout the environment, the organization creates redundancies that can deter or slow down attacks, giving security teams the necessary time to respond effectively. The significance of this strategy lies in its ability to adapt to evolving threats, addressing vulnerabilities at various levels and increasing the likelihood of thwarting attacks before they cause serious damage.

Layering security controls within an organization is a critical tactic in mitigating weaknesses and managing risks effectively. When security measures are implemented in layers, each layer adds a degree of complexity for potential attackers, making it harder for them to penetrate the system. For instance, combining firewalls with intrusion detection systems, access controls, and encryption ensures that if one layer is compromised, others remain intact to provide continuous protection. This segmented approach not only protects the integrity of the network but also makes it more challenging for unauthorized users to gain access to sensitive data. Moreover, by integrating these various security layers, organizations can fine-tune their defenses to suit specific threats, thus enhancing their agility in responding to incidents. Ultimately, this layered strategy not only helps in addressing immediate vulnerabilities but also cultivates a proactive security culture that encourages continual improvement and vigilance.

To effectively implement a defense in depth strategy, it is vital that all layers of security work seamlessly together, forming a cohesive defense network. Regular assessments and updates of security controls can ensure that they stay effective against emerging threats. Moreover, engaging in threat intelligence sharing can enhance situational awareness and reinforce collective security efforts across sectors. Emphasizing user awareness and training can also significantly bolster this strategy, as informed employees are often the first line of defense. Ultimately, building a dynamic and resilient security architecture rests on the foundation of defense in depth, preparing an organization not just to respond to threats but to anticipate and mitigate them well before they materialize.

4.2 Layered Security Controls

Within the defense in depth framework, various types of security controls are essential for establishing a robust security posture. Physical controls encompass tangible elements such as locks, security cameras, and access control systems that protect facilities and hardware. Technical controls involve the measures that protect the integrity of data and the systems used to process, store, and transmit it. Firewalls, intrusion detection systems, encryption protocols, and antivirus software serve this purpose by creating barriers against unauthorized access and malicious activities. Administrative controls refer to the policies, procedures, and training implemented to manage organizational security effectively. These controls guide employee behaviors, outline incident response plans, and ensure regulatory compliance, making them critical for fostering a security-conscious culture.

Integrating these layered security measures creates a comprehensive protection strategy against potential intrusions. Each layer of security acts as a net, catching threats at different stages of an attack. For instance, if a malicious actor bypasses physical controls, technical controls like firewalls and intrusion detection can thwart their progress further into the network. Similarly, administrative controls provide oversight and guidelines that define roles and responsibilities, ensuring that the technology and physical measures are effectively implemented. Practicing defense in depth allows organizations to create redundancies that dissuade attackers and mitigate risks. The interplay between these layers means that even if one control fails, others remain in place to catch security gaps, enhancing the overall resilience of the network.

It is crucial to monitor and routinely evaluate all layers of security to ensure their effectiveness. Regular audits and updates help identify weaknesses, outdated technologies, and process inefficiencies. Establishing a culture of continuous improvement in security protocols ensures that the controls in place can adapt to emerging threats and vulnerabilities. By cultivating an environment where security is everyone's responsibility, organizations can fortify their defenses against a myriad of cyber threats.

4.3 Role of Human Factors in Defense

Human behavior, training, and awareness are central to the effectiveness of security controls within a defense in depth strategy. Even the most sophisticated technological defenses can falter if the human element is not adequately addressed. People are often the weakest link in the security chain. For instance, a well-trained employee who understands the importance of adhering to security protocols is less likely to fall victim to phishing scams or other social engineering attacks. Conversely, even a single oversight—such as clicking on a malicious link—can expose an organization to significant risk. This highlights the importance of fostering a security-aware culture within an organization. Regular training sessions, continuous learning opportunities, and the promotion of open communication regarding security incidents can dramatically enhance overall security effectiveness. Moreover, awareness programs that emphasize the potential risks associated with human actions can lead to a more vigilant workforce, capable of recognizing threats before they escalate.

To effectively address human-related vulnerabilities, organizations should invest strategically in training and informed security practices. One approach is to implement a comprehensive security training program that goes beyond standard compliance measures, focusing instead on real-world scenarios and interactive learning. Simulated phishing campaigns can serve as practical exercises to help employees recognize suspicious communications and empower them to act appropriately. Additionally, integrating security into daily operations—such as encouraging employees to report potential threats without fear of reprimand—can significantly cultivate a resilient environment against cyber threats. It's not solely about conducting periodic training sessions; it's vital to create an ongoing dialogue about security within the workplace. Regular updates on emerging threats and changes in policies can ensure that security remains at the forefront of employees' minds, making them an active part of the organization's defense strategy.

Employing a human-centric approach to cybersecurity involves viewing employees not just as potential risks but as key assets in building resilience. Encouraging collaboration between IT security teams and various departments can enhance understanding and integration of security practices. This collaboration fosters a sense of ownership and accountability among employees, transforming them into proactive defenders of the organization's resources. As human factors play a pivotal role in cyber defense, organizations should continuously evaluate their training programs, adapting them to keep pace with evolving threats and the changing landscape of the work environment. A practical tip for enhancing human factors in defense is to incorporate gamification into training sessions, which can increase engagement and retention of critical security concepts, making the learning experience both informative and enjoyable.

Chapter 5: Risk Management in Cyber Security

5.1 Identifying and Classifying Risks

Identifying potential risks in the cybersecurity domain begins with a thorough methodology that emphasizes asset evaluation. Understanding what is at stake is foundational; organizations must first inventory their digital assets, including hardware, software, data, and even personnel. It is essential to assess the sensitivity and criticality of these assets to the organization's operations. This involves not only cataloging the assets but also analyzing how they are used, who uses them, and the potential impact of their compromise. Techniques such as threat modeling can be instrumental in this phase, allowing organizations to simulate various attack scenarios and identify vulnerabilities that could be exploited by adversaries. Additionally, employing frameworks like NIST's Cybersecurity Framework can streamline the risk identification process by offering a structured approach to identify, assess, and manage cybersecurity risks. A collaborative team approach, involving consultants, architects, and practitioners, ensures a comprehensive understanding of potential risks, as diverse expertise provides a more rounded perspective on what threats might be lurking and how to uncover them.

Once risks are identified, classifying them is crucial for effective prioritization and management. Risk classification systems serve as a useful tool for categorizing risks based on their nature and the consequences they may carry. One common approach is to categorize risks into categories such as environmental, technical, human, and operational. Each category can be further divided into subcategories that reflect specific threats, such as insider threats, malware, or natural disasters. By understanding the classification of each risk, organizations can prioritize which vulnerabilities to address first based on their likelihood of occurrence and potential impact. This prioritization process is aided by risk assessment methodologies that quantify the risk levels, which can help in aligning cybersecurity strategies with business objectives. For instance, risks that threaten critical assets or could lead to significant financial loss or reputational damage should be addressed more urgently compared to those with a lower impact or likelihood. Employing a systematic and analytical approach to classifying risks not only improves resource allocation but also supports the development of a robust defense strategy, ensuring that the most significant risks are managed swiftly and effectively.

Understanding the dynamics of risk identification and classification sets the stage for resilience in cybersecurity. By systematically evaluating assets and employing classification systems, organizations can better prepare themselves against evolving threats. Regular reviews of risk assessments, coupled with adapting classification systems to reflect changes in the threat landscape, can maintain the effectiveness of a cybersecurity program. It is beneficial to integrate insights gathered from incident responses and threat intelligence into the risk assessment process, as this allows for continuous improvement and adaptation. Practitioners should embrace a proactive mindset toward risk management, cultivating an environment of continuous assessment and adaptation to stay ahead of adversaries.

5.2 Risk Assessment Methodologies

Effective cyber risk assessment relies heavily on both quantitative and qualitative methodologies. Quantitative assessments involve the use of metrics and data analysis to evaluate risks based on mathematical models. This may include calculating potential losses from various scenarios, estimating the likelihood of cyber incidents based on historical data, and employing statistical techniques to assess vulnerabilities. Quantitative data provides a clear picture of financial impacts, enabling organizations to prioritize resources and make informed decisions based on objective evidence.

On the other hand, qualitative methodologies focus on non-numerical information, capturing the contextual factors surrounding risks. Techniques such as interviews, surveys, and expert judgments allow cybersecurity professionals to gain insights into the threat landscape. This approach helps in understanding the perceptions of stakeholders about potential risks and facilitating discussions around possible mitigations. By combining both methodologies, organizations can achieve a more comprehensive understanding of their cybersecurity posture, allowing for a balanced view that integrates data-driven insights with contextual factors.

Documenting findings from risk assessments plays a crucial role in informing stakeholders and guiding decision-making. Clear and concise documentation ensures that the results are accessible and understandable to all relevant personnel. Best practices in documentation include creating standardized templates for reporting, which streamline the process and make it easier to convey risks and recommendations effectively. Emphasizing clarity in language and visuals, such as risk heat maps and charts, can enhance stakeholder engagement. Furthermore, maintaining an ongoing risk register helps in tracking changes and updates over time, facilitating a dynamic approach to risk management. Regular reviews and communication of these findings to decision-makers enable organizations to adapt and strengthen their cybersecurity strategies, ultimately enhancing their resilience against potential threats.

A practical tip when conducting risk assessments is to incorporate stakeholder feedback throughout the process. This can create a more inclusive environment and ensure that various perspectives are considered, leading to a richer understanding of the risk landscape. Engaging different departments not only fosters a culture of security but also illuminates potential blind spots that may have been overlooked. This collaborative approach can significantly enhance the effectiveness of your risk assessments and improve overall cybersecurity posture.

5.3 Risk Mitigation Strategies

Effective risk mitigation strategies are fundamental for cybersecurity professionals, especially when addressing specific vulnerabilities within networks. Risk avoidance, for example, entails altering plans to sidestep potential risks altogether. This could mean not adopting a certain technology that has a known vulnerability or choosing not to engage in specific partnerships that could expose an organization to undue risk. On the other hand, risk reduction involves implementing measures that lessen the severity or likelihood of threats, such as deploying more robust security controls or conducting regular employee training to foster a culture of security awareness. Transferring risk is another strategy, often realized through cybersecurity insurance or outsourcing certain processes to third-party providers that can handle risks more effectively. Lastly, risk acceptance recognizes that some risks are unavoidable and can be tolerated within the organization's risk appetite, accompanied by careful monitoring and assessment to ensure such acceptance does not lead to damaging consequences.

The landscape of cybersecurity is not static, thus emphasizing the necessity for a dynamic risk management approach. As threats become more sophisticated and organizational priorities shift, strategies that once proved effective might become obsolete. Professionals must continuously assess and adjust their risk management frameworks, ensuring they remain aligned with current threat intelligence and business objectives. This might involve revisiting previously established risk assessments, updating security protocols, and maintaining strong communication channels across departments. Keeping abreast of industry trends and emerging technologies is vital, as it allows cybersecurity teams to foresee potential risks and adapt their strategies accordingly. Ultimately, a responsive approach enhances resilience, enabling organizations to withstand and recover from security incidents more effectively.

One practical tip for strengthening risk mitigation strategies is to establish a routine for evaluating the effectiveness of existing controls and risk management practices. This ongoing process helps identify new vulnerabilities and potential areas for improvement. Regularly scheduled reviews, combined with a culture of open communication, can empower teams to share insights about emerging threats and success stories similar to peer organizations, creating an environment where proactive risk management becomes embedded into the organizational fabric.

Chapter 6: Incident Response Planning

6.1 Planning and Preparation

An effective incident response plan is fundamental to an organization's ability to recover from cyber incidents while minimizing damage and restoring operations. The critical components of this plan include defining roles and responsibilities across the organizational hierarchy. Each team member, from executive leadership to IT staff, needs to clearly understand their specific duties during an incident. This clarity ensures a coordinated response where actions are not duplicated, and gaps in coverage are minimized. Resources must be allocated appropriately, including technologies, personnel, and access to external expertise when necessary. Compiling an updated inventory of assets, including hardware, software, and data critical to the organization, helps responders prioritize their focus based on impact assessment. Furthermore, incorporating communication strategies within the response plan is essential. It ensures that employees, stakeholders, and customers remain informed during an incident, which helps maintain trust and minimizes reputational damage.

The importance of conducting tabletop exercises cannot be understated in preparing teams for potential cyber incidents. These structured discussions simulate an incident scenario, allowing team members to walk through the response process in a controlled environment. This practice enables participants to understand their roles better, identify potential weaknesses in the plan, and enhance coordination among different departments. By exploring various scenarios, organizations can test their incident response strategies and promote a culture of preparedness. These exercises also serve to uncover any gaps in communication or resource allocation that may not be immediately apparent during regular operations. They provide teams with valuable insights into the complexities of incident response, preparing individuals not only on procedural steps but also on decision-making under pressure. This proactive approach contributes significantly to building resilience and fostering an environment where employees feel empowered to act decisively in the face of an incident.

Incorporating external feedback into the incident response plan can further strengthen a cyber security posture. Engaging with industry forums or security groups allows organizations to share experiences and learn from real-world incidents faced by others. This exposure to diverse perspectives and best practices often uncovers innovative strategies for improving incident response. Regularly updating the incident response plan is equally critical, tailoring it to account for evolving threats and technological advancements. Establishing a schedule for routine reviews and revisions ensures that the plan remains relevant and effectively meets the organization's needs. As cyber threats continue to evolve, maintaining a dynamic and responsive approach is essential for sustained resilience in network security.

6.2 Incident Detection and Analysis

Detecting cyber incidents effectively begins with deploying robust monitoring tools coupled with comprehensive threat intelligence. Organizations must utilize various monitoring solutions such as Security Information and Event Management (SIEM) systems, intrusion detection systems (IDS), and log management tools. These technologies play a crucial role in aggregating data from across the network to identify potential threats in real-time. Integrating threat intelligence enhances these tools by providing context around emerging threats, enabling security teams to prioritize alerts based on the relevance and severity of the threats. This proactive approach allows organizations to recognize anomalies and potential indicators of compromise before they escalate into serious incidents. By consistently refining their monitoring strategies and leveraging threat intelligence, organizations can enhance both their detection capabilities and the overall resilience of their infrastructure.

Once an incident is detected, the focus shifts to incident analysis techniques that facilitate a thorough understanding of the impact and root causes of the incident. Effective incident analysis begins with evidence collection and preservation, ensuring that logs and relevant data are intact for further examination. Techniques such as the Five Whys or the Fishbone Diagram can aid security teams in tracing back through the sequence of events that led to the incident. Establishing a timeline of events can be instrumental in understanding how the incident unfolded, the vulnerabilities exploited, and the initial entry point of the threat actor. Additionally, assessing the impact involves analyzing the extent of data loss, service disruption, and any regulatory implications that may arise. This comprehensive approach not only uncovers the root cause but also informs subsequent mitigation strategies, ensuring that organizations can improve their defenses and prevent similar occurrences in the future.

In the realm of incident management, the value of maintaining a thorough documentation process cannot be overstated. Keeping detailed records of incidents, response actions taken, and lessons learned helps organizations refine their security posture over time. This historical data serves as a valuable reference for future incidents, enabling security professionals to recognize patterns and develop more effective incident response plans. Continuous improvement should be at the forefront of incident detection and analysis strategies, allowing organizations to evolve their defenses in an ever-changing threat landscape. Employing regular training and simulations also prepares teams for real-world incidents, enhancing their response capabilities and ensuring that they can operate effectively under pressure.

6.3 Post-Incident Recovery and Lessons Learned

Recovery after an incident is a critical phase that heavily influences an organization's ability to respond swiftly and effectively to future challenges. Establishing clear and structured communication with stakeholders and impacted parties is paramount during this phase. This includes identifying and contacting key individuals, organizations, and teams that have been affected by the incident, ensuring they are updated on recovery efforts and timelines. Transparent communication helps build trust and prevents misinformation from spreading, which can complicate recovery. Stakeholders should be kept informed of the progress, the challenges facing recovery efforts, and any additional resources that may be required. By providing regular updates and facilitating discussions, organizations can foster a collaborative atmosphere, which is essential for a collective recovery process.

Capturing lessons learned from an incident is equally important, as it enables organizations to enhance future incident response strategies and resilience. After the dust settles, teams should conduct thorough reviews of what happened, the response actions taken, and the effectiveness of those actions. This includes documenting successes, identifying gaps, and recognizing areas where response plans may need adjustment. Engaging all relevant parties in this reflection ensures diverse perspectives are captured, adding depth to the analysis. Furthermore, maintaining this repository of lessons learned can serve as valuable training material for new team members and a reference point for enhancing security postures. By continually updating incident response protocols based on past experiences, organizations not only enhance their immediate responses but also build a culture of resilience that prepares them for unforeseen future incidents.

Emphasizing the importance of both effective communication and the diligent documentation of lessons learned allows organizations to emerge from incidents not only with a restored operational capacity but also strengthened resilience. This proactive approach lays a foundation for future preparedness, enabling teams to not only react to cyber threats but to anticipate and mitigate potential risks before they escalate. As you assess your organization's incident response mechanism, remember that the work does not end once the immediate crisis is resolved. Regularly revisit your documentation and communication strategies to ensure they evolve alongside the ever-changing landscape of cybersecurity threats.

Chapter 7: Integrating Security Across the Network

7.1 Network Segmentation and Micro-segmentation

Network segmentation is a crucial strategy employed by organizations to minimize their attack surfaces. By dividing a network into smaller, manageable segments, security professionals can limit access and exposure of sensitive resources. This approach not only helps in containing potential breaches but also improves performance and simplifies regulatory compliance. When segments are properly defined, potential threats can be isolated, preventing attackers from moving freely across the network. This layered defense is vital in today's threat landscape, where the complexity and sophistication of attacks are constantly evolving.

Micro-segmentation enhances traditional segmentation by going a step further to isolate workloads and applications within each segment. This technique involves creating secure zones within a data center or cloud environment, allowing for granular control over traffic flows. By implementing policies that restrict communication between different workloads based on specific criteria, organizations can significantly reduce lateral movement. Should an attacker gain access to one part of the network, micro-segmentation hinders their ability to explore and exploit other areas. In practice, this ensures that even if a breach occurs, the impact is restricted solely to a small section of the network.

To effectively implement network segmentation and micro-segmentation, practitioners should ensure they have a thorough understanding of their network topology and asset inventory. Regularly reviewing and updating segmentation policies is essential as organizational needs and threat landscapes change. Furthermore, integrating these strategies within a broader defense-in-depth approach significantly bolsters overall security and resilience, making it harder for adversaries to infiltrate and operate undetected within the network.

7.2 Secure Configuration Management

Secure configuration management revolves around the principle of establishing and maintaining computer systems in a state that minimizes vulnerabilities. Misconfigurations can occur due to oversight, lack of knowledge, or even simple human error, potentially leading to severe security breaches. The foundation of secure configuration management involves understanding the baseline of system configurations, hardening them against potential attacks, and regularly reviewing and updating these configurations as necessary. This process ensures that both hardware and software components operate according to the best security practices, drastically reducing the attack surface for any given IT environment. Implementing least privilege principles, ensuring that machines and applications have only the necessary permissions, and regularly validating configurations against known security benchmarks or frameworks, such as CIS Controls or NIST standards, are essential practices to achieve a fortified configuration stance.

To bolster these manual processes, a variety of automated tools and practices play a crucial role in maintaining secure configurations across IT environments. Tools such as configuration management software, vulnerability scanners, and compliance monitoring systems automate the monitoring and enforcement of security settings. These technologies enable security teams to detect deviations from the established norms in real-time, thereby allowing for immediate corrective actions. Indeed, leveraging automation not only streamlines the task of configuration management but also ensures consistency in applying crucial updates and patches across diverse systems. Integration of tools that support Infrastructure as Code (IaC) can also help establish a repeatable and predictable model for configurations, further enhancing resilience and responsiveness to potential threats. By employing such systems, organizations can achieve a higher level of operational efficiency and significantly reduce the risks posed by misconfigurations.

A practical takeaway for cybersecurity professionals is the importance of establishing a culture of security awareness throughout the organization, emphasizing the role of secure configurations in the broader context of operational security. This can involve regular training and updates to ensure that all team members understand the significance of secure configuration management and are equipped with the knowledge to recognize and prevent potential misconfigurations. Maintaining an ongoing dialogue about cybersecurity threats, along with the regular use of automated tools for monitoring and configuration management, will reinforce a proactive stance towards maintaining security in complex IT environments.

7.3 Continuous Monitoring and Logging

Real-time monitoring and logging are crucial components of a robust cybersecurity strategy. They empower organizations to quickly identify and respond to threats, minimizing potential damage. The ability to detect anomalies as they occur allows security teams to address vulnerabilities before they escalate into significant breaches. Continuous monitoring provides visibility across the entire network, enabling organizations to recognize unusual behavior patterns that may signal an attack. In today's fast-paced digital environment, where threats can evolve rapidly, having a proactive approach through real-time logging means that security incidents can be managed before they lead to major compromises.

Configuring logging policies effectively is essential to maximize visibility while avoiding overwhelming analysts with noise. One best practice is to define clear objectives for what needs to be logged based on the specific threats pertinent to your environment. Prioritizing log sources can streamline the analysis process, ensuring that attention is focused on the most critical areas. For instance, while detailed logs from endpoint security systems are invaluable, excessive data from non-critical applications can lead to analyst fatigue and missed alerts. By employing log aggregation tools and leveraging correlation techniques, organizations can distill vast volumes of data into actionable insights. This approach not only enhances the efficiency of response teams but also significantly improves the overall security posture of the organization.

Finally, implementing automated alert systems can further enhance the effectiveness of logging practices. By utilizing machine learning algorithms, organizations can filter false positives and highlight genuine threats, ensuring that analysts spend their time on what matters most. Regularly reviewing and recalibrating log settings is equally important, as threat landscapes are constantly changing. These adjustments ensure that monitoring remains relevant and efficient, adapting to both evolving threats and organizational changes. In an era where the complexity of networks is ever-increasing, maintaining a strategic approach to continuous monitoring and logging will bolster resilience and protect valuable assets.

Chapter 8: Building a Cyber Resilient Culture

8.1 Employee Training and Awareness Programs

A well-rounded approach to employee training is crucial in establishing a culture of security awareness within any organization. Comprehensive training programs serve as the foundation for cultivating an environment where security is everyone's responsibility. This shift in mindset ensures that employees understand their roles in protecting sensitive information and are equipped with the knowledge to identify and respond to security threats effectively. When employees are educated about the potential risks they face, ranging from phishing attacks to data breaches, they become active participants in the defense of the organization's assets. Fostering this culture of security awareness not only mitigates risks but also empowers employees to take ownership of their security practices, leading to reduced vulnerabilities across the organization.

Engaging training methodologies play a vital role in ensuring that security best practices are retained and applied effectively by employees. Traditional training methods, such as lengthy presentations and static materials, often fail to capture employees' attention, leading to diminished knowledge retention. Innovative approaches like gamification, interactive simulations, and scenario-based learning can significantly enhance engagement. For instance, using game-like environments to simulate real-life security challenges allows employees to practice decision-making in a risk-free setting. This hands-on experience reinforces learning and enables employees to remember crucial security practices. Incorporating regular assessments and feedback mechanisms into training programs not only helps reinforce knowledge but also creates opportunities for continuous improvement, helping employees stay updated with evolving security threats and best practices.

It's essential to understand that training should not be a one-time event but rather an ongoing process that evolves alongside the threat landscape. Creating a robust training program that accommodates new threats and incorporates feedback from employees can lead to a more resilient organization. Additionally, integrating training with regular security updates and discussions can keep security top-of-mind for all employees. By establishing clear channels for reporting incidents and encouraging open communication, organizations can further enhance their training efforts, making security a seamless aspect of the organizational culture. Regularly emphasizing the importance of security awareness and providing employees with the tools and knowledge they need can lead to a safer and more secure workplace.

8.2 Encouraging Reporting and Transparency

Open communication serves as a cornerstone for fostering an environment where employees feel empowered and encouraged to report suspicious activities. Cybersecurity incidents can be disconcerting; hence, when an organization cultivates a culture of transparency and support around reporting, it alleviates the fear of repercussions among staff. Employees are more likely to come forward with their concerns when they believe their voices will be heard and valued. This sense of security can be enhanced by clear communication from leadership regarding the importance of vigilance in matters of cybersecurity. Training programs that emphasize the role of individuals in the collective security effort can further instill a sense of responsibility and encourage proactive involvement in identifying potential risks. Furthermore, providing multiple avenues for reporting, whether through anonymous hotlines, direct communication with management, or designated cybersecurity representatives, creates a more inclusive atmosphere. In this way, organizations can benefit from employees' insights while also enabling early detection of suspicious activities.

Establishing frameworks for transparency in how incidents are handled is crucial for building trust within an organization. When employees understand how reports are processed and the outcomes of incidents, they can more effectively assess the seriousness with which the organization approaches cybersecurity. Regular updates about incidents, including what has been learned and how policies might change in response, signal to employees that transparency is a priority. This approach involves not only documenting incidents but also communicating insights gained to the workforce. Transparency in incident handling contributes to a learning culture where all members can see the direct impact of their contributions. Organizations can implement incident response hotlines or regular briefings following an incident to share lessons learned and improvements made. Such practices help demystify the incident response process and encourage participation while mitigating feelings of fear and uncertainty surrounding potential vulnerabilities.

Incorporating a feedback loop into the reporting process ensures that employees feel their contributions matter. After a report is made, updating the reporting individual about the actions taken can bolster trust and reinforce the notion that their concerns have led to meaningful changes. This can be further supported by actively seeking input on the reporting process itself, allowing employees to express what reporting channels feel most comfortable or effective for them. Ultimately, fostering a culture where open communication and transparent incident handling are prioritized not only enhances reporting rates but also strengthens the overall resilience of the organization against threats. Organizations should consider implementing annual reviews of their communication strategies and incident management processes to adapt to evolving threats and employee needs, thereby promoting a proactive cybersecurity environment.

8.3 Leadership and Governance in Cyber Resilience

Leadership plays a critical role in establishing a cyber-resilient culture within an organization. Effective leaders understand that their vision sets the tone for the entire cybersecurity posture. They must articulate a clear and compelling vision of what cyber resilience looks like, ensuring that it aligns with the organization's broader goals. This vision should encompass a commitment to security that permeates every level of the organization, fostering an environment where cybersecurity is prioritized. By demonstrating strong support for security initiatives, leaders inspire staff to take part in creating a culture that values resilience. Resources must be allocated wisely to equip teams with the necessary tools and training, ensuring that employees at all levels are prepared to respond to cyber threats. When leaders prioritize cyber resilience, they not only safeguard their organization's assets but also empower employees to own their role in maintaining security, thus enhancing the overall posture against cyber threats.

Governance structures must be implemented to reinforce the importance of cyber resilience across all organizational levels. This begins with establishing clear roles and responsibilities, ensuring that cybersecurity is a shared priority rather than the task of a single department. A robust governance framework might include a cybersecurity committee that reports directly to the executive team, incorporating representatives from various departments to ensure a cross-functional approach. By embedding cyber resilience in the organization's governance, including risk appetite and regulatory compliance, leaders can ensure that cybersecurity strategies are not just reactive but also proactive.

Organizations should conduct regular reviews of their governance structures to adapt to the ever-evolving cyber threat landscape, ensuring that policies and practices remain effective and relevant.

Creating a lasting culture of cyber resilience requires continuous effort and adaptation. Cybersecurity professionals should advocate for regular training and awareness programs that keep staff informed about the latest threats and best practices. Building relationships across teams fosters collaboration and knowledge sharing, which is essential in a landscape where threats may rapidly evolve. Sharing success stories of resilience within the organization can motivate all levels of staff, reinforcing the idea that everyone is a vital contributor to the cybersecurity effort. By integrating leadership commitment and governance into the fabric of the organization, cyber resilience becomes not just a goal, but a fundamental aspect of the organization's identity.

Chapter 9: Developing Cyber Resilience Metrics

9.1 Key Performance Indicators for Cyber Resilience

Identifying essential Key Performance Indicators (KPIs) is crucial for understanding an organization's cyber resilience posture. KPIs serve as measurable values that help organizations assess their ability to withstand, respond to, and recover from cyber threats. Some important KPIs might include the time taken to detect threats, the number of incidents that go undetected, the frequency of security audits, and the average time to recover from disruptions. Monitoring these metrics enables organizations to gain insights into their vulnerability areas, allowing them to prioritize resources for security enhancements. Additionally, KPIs should also encompass employee training metrics, such as the percentage of staff that completed security awareness programs, which is vital since human error can often be a significant vulnerability in cyber defense.

Aligning metrics with organizational goals is imperative to illustrate the value of cyber resilience initiatives. When KPIs are mapped to strategic business objectives, they provide a context that makes the data more relevant and actionable. For instance, if a company's goal is to ensure 99.9% service uptime, relevant KPIs might include the mean time to recovery after an incident and the number of successful threats mitigated that could disrupt services. This alignment not only aids in justifying investments in cybersecurity measures but also helps communicate cyber resilience efforts in terms that are meaningful to stakeholders. By demonstrating how improved cyber resilience supports overall business goals, organizations can foster greater commitment and support for their cybersecurity initiatives.

A practical approach to developing effective KPIs for cyber resilience involves continuous iteration and adjustment. The cyber threat landscape is ever-evolving, and so should be the metrics used to measure resilience. Routine reviews of the KPIs in place, based on emerging threats and changes in organizational priorities, can ensure that the metrics remain relevant and impactful. This proactive stance not only strengthens the organization's defenses but also instills a culture of resilience throughout the workforce, making everyone a stakeholder in the cyber security landscape.

9.2 Monitoring and Evaluating Metrics

Continuous monitoring of resilience metrics is critical for enabling timely decision-making and adjustments within cybersecurity frameworks. Organizations can adopt various techniques, such as real-time data collection, automated alerting systems, and dashboard visualizations. These tools enable cybersecurity professionals to keep track of key performance indicators (KPIs) related to network resilience. By leveraging automated scripts and monitoring solutions that analyze traffic patterns and system behaviors, teams can detect anomalies that may indicate potential vulnerabilities or breaches. Regular reviews of these metrics not only help identify weaknesses in existing defenses but also guide the strategic allocation of resources to improve resilience. Empirical data gathered through continuous monitoring maintains an updated profile of the network, which is essential for rapid response to threats, ensuring a proactive rather than reactive security posture.

Evaluating the effectiveness of resilience initiatives based on performance data requires a methodical approach that blends qualitative and quantitative analysis. One effective methodology involves setting clear objectives at the outset, ensuring that each resilience initiative has measurable outcomes. After implementation, ongoing analysis of these objectives against collected metrics provides insights into successes and areas needing improvement. Techniques such as benchmarking against industry standards and conducting post-incident reviews can yield valuable lessons, allowing teams to refine their strategies. Engaging in simulation exercises or tabletop drills allows for real-world testing of resilience plans, revealing practical shortcomings that might not surface during standard evaluations. This comprehensive approach honors the intricacies of cybersecurity environments and underscores the importance of adaptability as threats evolve.

Investing in robust monitoring and evaluation frameworks equips cybersecurity professionals with the intelligence necessary to enhance network resilience. The integration of data-driven insights into the resilience planning process not only fortifies defense mechanisms but also fosters a culture of continuous improvement. Tools such as regular audits and stakeholder feedback loops can solidify an organization's position in the increasingly complex cybersecurity landscape. By maintaining a dynamic approach to monitoring and evaluation, teams can not only react to current threats but also anticipate future challenges, fundamentally transforming their cybersecurity posture.

9.3 Reporting and Communicating Metrics to Stakeholders

Effectively communicating resilience metrics is crucial for engaging various stakeholders, especially in the realm of cyber security. Different audiences have varying levels of technical expertise, which necessitates tailored strategies to convey the importance and impact of cyber resilience initiatives. For technical audiences, detailed statistical analyses and technical jargon may be appropriate, as they can appreciate the complexities and nuances involved. However, for non-technical stakeholders, such as executives or board members, it's vital to distill these metrics into clear, actionable language that focuses on risk, compliance, and the overall organizational mission. Utilizing visual aids like dashboards and infographics can bridge the gap between complex data and straightforward messaging, making it easier for all stakeholders to grasp the significance of the metrics being presented. A narrative approach that connects resilience efforts to business outcomes can enhance engagement, thereby fostering a culture of awareness and support for cyber resilience initiatives.

Reporting frameworks significantly influence how stakeholders perceive and support cyber resilience efforts. Various frameworks provide structured methodologies for presenting resilience metrics, which can not only clarify the data but also frame it within broader organizational goals. For instance, a framework that emphasizes risk management may highlight vulnerabilities and their potential impact on business operations, prompting stakeholders to consider resilience as a fundamental aspect of risk governance. Additionally, standardized reporting frameworks, like the NIST Cybersecurity Framework or ISO 27001, offer a common language and set of expectations that help unify understanding across diverse stakeholder groups. By aligning with these recognized frameworks, cyber security professionals can enhance credibility and encourage a more robust investment in resilience initiatives. This alignment not only assures stakeholders about compliance and accountability but also signals to them that the organization is committed to maintaining a strong security posture.

Incorporating storytelling into reporting can also amplify its effectiveness. Narratives that outline real-world examples of resilience practices in action—such as a successful incident response or a near-miss that was effectively mitigated—can leave a lasting impact on stakeholders and drive home the importance of proactive measures. Such stories can personalize the metrics, making them more relatable and compelling. Ultimately, the persistent challenge is to translate resilience metrics into insights that resonate with each stakeholder group. Cyber security professionals are encouraged to engage in continuous dialogues with their audiences, solicit feedback, and refine their communication strategies accordingly. This adaptive approach will not only improve understanding but also promote a shared commitment to enhancing cyber resilience across the organization.

Chapter 10: Technology Solutions for Cyber Resilience

10.1 Security Tools and Technologies Overview

Various security tools are essential in enhancing cyber resilience, each serving a unique role in protecting an organization's digital assets. Firewalls act as the first line of defense, monitoring incoming and outgoing traffic based on predetermined security rules. They can be hardware-based, software-based, or a combination of both, thus providing flexible options depending on the organization's needs. Intrusion Detection Systems (IDS) complement firewalls by monitoring network traffic for suspicious activity and potential threats. They analyze patterns to detect anomalies, providing alerts for incidents that may require further investigation.

Integrating these technologies fosters a cohesive defense strategy that enhances an organization's overall security posture. For instance, combining firewalls with Intrusion Prevention Systems (IPS) can enable more proactive defense mechanisms, as IPS can take immediate action to block detected threats. This synergy between tools ensures that multiple layers of protection are in place, which is a fundamental principle of defense in depth. Employing supplier assurance is another critical component. By ensuring that third-party vendors adhere to stringent security measures, organizations can significantly reduce the risk posed by external partnerships. In an interconnected environment, a holistic approach that integrates various security tools and practices is vital for defeating increasingly sophisticated cyber threats.

As professionals working in the field of cybersecurity, it is crucial to stay informed about the latest advancements in security technologies. Regularly assessing and updating the tools you deploy in your organization can drastically enhance your defenses. Remember that no tool is a silver bullet; instead, the combination and interplay of multiple security technologies create robust defenses that can withstand the rapidly evolving threat landscape.

10.2 Integrating Automation and AI

The integration of automation and artificial intelligence (AI) stands to revolutionize the field of cybersecurity significantly. By enhancing incident detection capabilities, organizations can respond more swiftly to emerging threats, thus mitigating potential damage. Automation tools equipped with AI algorithms can analyze vast datasets in real-time, identifying patterns that may indicate malicious activities. This capability accelerates the detection process well beyond human capacity, allowing cybersecurity teams to focus their efforts on more strategic initiatives. Moreover, through automated responses to specific types of incidents, not only can response times be significantly reduced, but the risk of human error can also be minimized. When systems automatically initiate predefined responses to threats, the likelihood of oversight or delayed reaction from human operators diminishes, further strengthening an organization's defenses against cyber threats.

Implementing AI-driven solutions within existing cyber resilience frameworks requires thoughtful consideration of several practical aspects. Cybersecurity professionals must evaluate the compatibility of new technologies with current systems and processes to ensure seamless operational continuity. Risk assessment is crucial during this integration phase to address any potential vulnerabilities that new tools may introduce. Additionally, adequate training for personnel is vital, as the effectiveness of AI systems depends heavily on how well operators understand and manage these complex technologies. This includes cultivating a culture of collaboration between human teams and AI systems, ensuring that the automated responses complement human decision-making rather than replace it. Balancing automation with human oversight allows for intelligent responses while retaining accountability and adaptability amidst evolving cyber threats.

As organizations continue to navigate the integration of automation and AI into their cyber resilience strategies, keeping abreast of industry best practices and emerging technologies is essential. Sharing insights and learning from peer experiences can provide valuable perspectives on challenges and solutions that have been encountered, thus facilitating a smoother transition into more automated environments. Cultivating open lines of communication with technology vendors can also yield beneficial information about the capabilities and limitations of AI solutions, guiding informed choices that bolster overall network defenses.

10.3 Future Technologies in Cyber Resilience

Emerging technologies such as blockchain and quantum computing are reshaping the landscape of cyber resilience. Blockchain offers a decentralized approach to data management, enhancing security by eliminating single points of failure. The immutability of blockchain records creates an environment where data integrity is paramount, making it difficult for malicious actors to alter information without detection. Cybersecurity professionals are recognizing the potential of blockchain not only in securing transactions but also in implementing robust data verification processes across supply chains. Additionally, the advent of quantum computing poses both challenges and opportunities. While it holds the potential to break traditional encryption methods, it simultaneously paves the way for new quantum-resistant algorithms, which can dramatically enhance our capacity to safeguard sensitive information. As these technologies mature, their integration into cyber resilience strategies may not only mitigate existing risks but also prepare organizations for future challenges.

Staying updated with technological advancements can provide a significant competitive edge in resilience planning. Organizations that actively pursue knowledge about emerging technologies can refine their security frameworks, making them more adaptable to changing threat landscapes. Engaging in continuous learning allows professionals to anticipate potential vulnerabilities introduced by new tech trends and to leverage advancements for preventive measures. By incorporating insights gained from cutting-edge research and development, cybersecurity teams can implement innovative solutions to enhance their defenses. This proactive stance fosters a culture of resilience, where adaptation and evolution become core competencies. Furthermore, organizations that invest in training their workforce on these advancements not only strengthen their overall security posture but also cultivate a team capable of identifying and mitigating risks effectively. The commitment to leveraging future technologies can ultimately transform how organizations approach cyber resilience.

Incorporating emerging technologies into resilience strategies is not merely an option; it is a necessity for organizations seeking a secure future. It is essential to analyze how these innovations can be woven into existing frameworks while remaining agile enough to pivot when new threats arise. Collaboration with technology experts and staying connected with industry trends allow cybersecurity professionals to stay ahead of the curve. Fostering such an adaptive mindset empowers teams, enabling them to embrace technological changes rather than resist them. Holistically integrating future technologies could very well be the cornerstone of a resilient cyber infrastructure. Prioritize ongoing education to ensure your team is well-equipped to navigate the complexities introduced by these advancements.

Chapter 11: Compliance and Regulatory Considerations

11.1 Relevant Cybersecurity Regulations

There are several key cybersecurity regulations that significantly impact organizations across various sectors. The General Data Protection Regulation (GDPR) is a comprehensive data protection law in the European Union that mandates businesses to protect the personal data and privacy of EU citizens for transactions that occur within EU member states. It imposes strict guidelines on the collection, storage, and processing of personal data, making organizations accountable for breaches and requiring them to implement appropriate security measures. Similarly, the Health Insurance Portability and Accountability Act (HIPAA) sets standards for protecting sensitive patient information in the healthcare field. It requires healthcare providers, payers, and partners like vendors to safeguard electronic health information, establishing clear privacy and security rules to prevent unauthorized access. Compliance with these regulations not only helps organizations avoid legal penalties but also builds trust with clients and stakeholders.

Understanding the regulatory landscape is crucial for cybersecurity professionals, as it serves as a foundation upon which resilience strategies are built. Regulations provide a framework for identifying potential risks and implementing defenses that align with compliance requirements. Navigating these regulations allows organizations to enhance their security posture by incorporating best practices tailored to meet specific obligations. For instance, if a company deals with health data, knowing HIPAA provisions helps prioritize security measures around data integrity and confidentiality. Recently, organizations have begun integrating concepts like Supplier Assurance and Defence in Depth into their resilience strategies, recognizing that a strong cybersecurity framework requires collaboration and layers of defense. By comprehensively assessing regulatory obligations, security professionals can better shape their cybersecurity initiatives, ensuring that their networks are not only compliant but also resilient against evolving threats.

For professionals in the field, staying updated on evolving regulations and compliance standards is essential. Engaging with legal experts and participating in training programs can enhance understanding and facilitate better implementation of compliance measures. Regular workshops and webinars can provide valuable insights into the implications of new regulations, allowing cybersecurity teams to adapt their strategies effectively. Furthermore, maintaining an open line of communication with stakeholders regarding compliance can foster a culture of security and trust throughout the organization, enhancing overall resilience.

11.2 Compliance Strategies and Best Practices

Achieving compliance while ensuring resilience capabilities and maintaining operational efficiency requires a strategic approach. Organizations must first understand the nuances of their compliance obligations, which often involve regulations that can vary widely by industry and region. To build a solid foundation, companies can adopt a layered defense strategy: integrating compliance into every aspect of their cybersecurity framework rather than treating it as an isolated requirement. This encourages teams to identify the interdependencies between compliance requirements and operational processes. For instance, when implementing security controls, it is essential to select solutions that not only meet compliance criteria but also enhance the overall security posture. Therefore, adopting an agile framework that promotes continuous improvement is crucial. Cybersecurity teams should engage in regular discussions with compliance officers to align security measures with organizational goals without stifling innovation or agility.

Regular audits and updates to compliance frameworks are paramount in navigating the fast-evolving landscape of regulations. Cybersecurity professionals should establish a schedule for periodic reviews of compliance policies and procedures, ensuring that they reflect current laws and best practices. Implementing automated tools can streamline this process, helping to track compliance status across various domains efficiently. Additionally, engaging with industry peers can shed light on emerging trends and regulatory expectations, providing valuable insights for necessary adjustments. Training and awareness programs are also vital, as ensuring all employees are informed about compliance requirements fosters a culture of accountability and vigilance. As regulations change, it may also be beneficial to develop a quick-response team that can address compliance challenges swiftly, ensuring that the organization remains adaptable and resilient amidst the shifting landscape.

Incorporating compliance strategies seamlessly into the organizational fabric enhances resilience and helps avoid pitfalls associated with non-compliance. Regularly updating compliance frameworks and conducting thorough audits may seem labor-intensive, but the investment pays off significantly in safeguarding the organization's reputation and financial stability. As you navigate these processes, consider using a risk-based approach to prioritize compliance activities based on the potential impact on your organization and its stakeholders. A focus on continuous education and engagement with all levels of staff can amplify a unified approach to adherence and security, ultimately creating a more resilient cybersecurity environment.

11.3 Balancing Compliance and Resilience

The relationship between compliance and resilience is fundamental to the security architecture of any organization. Compliance often focuses on adhering to established laws, regulations, and standards, which can create a structured environment for security practices. However, resilience goes beyond mere compliance; it involves creating an adaptable infrastructure capable of withstanding and recovering from incidents. To effectively align these two objectives, organizations must recognize that compliance requirements can serve as a foundation for building resilience. For instance, adhering to GDPR or HIPAA can ensure the protection of sensitive data, which enhances an organization's ability to respond to breaches. By integrating compliance into the fabric of operational resilience, organizations can foster an environment where security measures are not only about ticking boxes but also about genuinely protecting assets and maintaining trust with stakeholders.

To evaluate compliance needs while ensuring a robust security posture, organizations can adopt a framework based on continuous assessment and improvement. Start by conducting a thorough risk assessment that identifies both compliance obligations and potential vulnerabilities within the network. This dual approach allows organizations to map compliance requirements directly to their security initiatives. Implementing a risk management program can help prioritize compliance activities based on their potential impact on resilience. Organizations should also incorporate regular training and awareness programs that align compliance with best practices in cyber hygiene. By fostering a culture that values both compliance and proactive security, organizations can create a more resilient infrastructure. Tools such as automated compliance checks and integrated security monitoring can also enhance this framework, enabling organizations to adapt swiftly to evolving threats while meeting regulatory standards.

For cyber security professionals, this synergy between compliance and resilience is not merely a theoretical exercise but a practical necessity. As organizations face increasing cyber threats and regulatory pressures, the ability to swiftly incorporate compliance into the security strategy will prove invaluable. Regularly revisiting the alignment of compliance with resilience goals allows organizations to stay ahead of potential risks while fostering a secure environment for operations. Utilizing metrics to measure both compliance and the effectiveness of resilience strategies can guide decision-making processes, ensuring that resources are effectively utilized. By incorporating feedback loops from security incidents into compliance policies, organizations can enhance their defenses and reinforce their commitment to both compliance and resilience.

Chapter 12: Business Continuity and Cyber Resilience

12.1 Designing a Business Continuity Plan

An effective business continuity plan (BCP) is essential for organizations looking to enhance their cyber resilience. At its core, a BCP must outline critical components such as risk assessment, incident response, recovery strategies, and continuous improvement. The risk assessment identifies potential threats, vulnerabilities, and the business's impact, allowing organizations to prioritize what matters most. Following this, a clear incident response plan should delineate roles, responsibilities, and escalation procedures during a cyber incident, ensuring swift action is taken. Recovery strategies need to focus on how to restore operations rapidly, including backup procedures and alternative communication methods that will sustain business functions. Importantly, regular training and awareness programs are vital to keep employees informed about their roles within the BCP. Testing the plan through simulations can reveal weaknesses and areas for improvement, embedding resilience into the organization's core operations.

Despite the best intentions, many organizations fall into common pitfalls when crafting their BCPs. One major issue is developing a plan in isolation, neglecting to involve key stakeholders across all departments. Collaboration ensures the plan reflects diverse perspectives and operational realities. Another frequent oversight is the failure to regularly update the BCP to align with technological advancements or changes within the business, leading to outdated or ineffective strategies. To counter these challenges, organizations should institute a regular review cycle for BCP updates that coincides with broader business reviews or after significant incidents. Additionally, prioritizing awareness and training can help avert complacency, as familiarity breeds gaps in readiness. Finally, avoiding the temptation to overcomplicate the plan can greatly enhance its effectiveness. A streamlined, clear, and actionable BCP is more likely to be successfully implemented during a crisis.

Always remember that a business continuity plan is not a one-time effort but an ongoing process of adaptation and growth. Regularly engaging with the latest trends in cyber threats and resilience can significantly enhance your organization's preparedness. Consider aligning your BCP with established frameworks or standards, such as ISO 22301 or the NIST Cybersecurity Framework, to ensure your strategies not only meet compliance requirements but are also recognized best practices in risk management. By integrating business continuity efforts with supplier assurance and a defense-in-depth strategy, organizations can cultivate a fortified environment that inherently supports both operational continuity and resilience against cyber threats.

12.2 Testing and Exercising Business Continuity Plans

Regularly testing and updating business continuity plans is essential for maintaining their effectiveness and relevance. Methodologies for conducting these tests vary widely but should reflect the specific risks and challenges faced by an organization. One effective approach is to incorporate a cycle of review and adjustment, where plans are evaluated at predetermined intervals or following significant changes in business operations or the threat landscape. This understanding allows for the identification of gaps in the plans and helps ensure the incorporation of lessons learned from both internal experiences and external incidents. Utilizing techniques such as tabletop exercises, where key stakeholders come together to walk through scenarios, can highlight weaknesses in processes and communication. Moreover, employing automated testing tools can help simulate attacks or failures in real time, revealing how systems and personnel respond under pressure, leading to more comprehensive updates based on empirical data.

Conducting exercises that simulate real-world incidents is vital for assessing preparedness. These simulations, whether table-top exercises or full-scale drills, serve to immerse team members in scenarios resembling potential threats, whether cyber-attacks, natural disasters, or operational interruptions. Engaging in these drills not only validates the business continuity plans but also fosters a culture of readiness within the team. Realistic simulations allow participants to practice their roles, refine communication strategies, and reinforce their understanding of procedures during a crisis. This practice minimizes panic and confusion should a real incident occur. Integration with broader organizational emergency response initiatives further enhances resilience, ensuring that all aspects of risk management and recovery are aligned and operational. Regular debriefs following these exercises facilitate shared learning, allowing teams to continuously improve protocols based on observed performance and feedback.

Ultimately, actively maintaining and testing business continuity plans is a crucial investment in organizational resilience. Cybersecurity professionals should advocate for a culture of continuous improvement, where lessons learned are not merely noted but actively integrated into practice. This proactive stance helps organizations adapt to a constantly evolving threat landscape, ensuring that they are not only prepared to respond to incidents but also capable of recovering swiftly and effectively, safeguarding their operations and reputation.

12.3 Alignment with Cyber Resilience Goals

Business continuity planning must be intricately woven into cyber resilience goals to ensure a comprehensive approach to organizational protection. Cyber threats are evolving at an unprecedented rate, and the impact of such vulnerabilities extends beyond mere data loss. A successful cyber resilience strategy integrates business continuity procedures that prepare organizations for potential cyber incidents while ensuring ongoing operations. This integration begins with risk assessments that identify key assets and potential threats, allowing teams to synchronize their business continuity strategies with cyber resilience objectives. By aligning recovery time and recovery point objectives with the organization's overall risk appetite, teams can prioritize critical functions and establish effective incident response plans that support both resilience and continuity.

Examining real-world case studies provides practical insights into the synergy between business continuity and cyber resilience. For instance, a major financial institution experienced a ransomware incident that temporarily halted its operations. By having already established a robust business continuity plan that included fortified cyber defenses, the institution was able to restore services within a few hours, significantly mitigating potential financial losses. Similarly, a healthcare provider implemented a dual-focused strategy, integrating cyber resilience metrics into its emergency management processes. During a cybersecurity breach that jeopardized sensitive patient data, the preemptive business continuity measures allowed for uninterrupted patient care, demonstrating the value of such integration. These examples highlight how organizations can effectively navigate cyber threats while maintaining their operational integrity through well-aligned resilience and continuity frameworks.

One practical approach for cybersecurity professionals is to establish a cross-disciplinary team involving both IT and business continuity experts. Regular workshops can facilitate the sharing of knowledge about potential threats and operational impacts, ensuring that both domains understand their interdependencies. This collaboration fosters a culture of resilience throughout the organization, enhancing not only the current processes but also the overall readiness to adapt to emerging cybersecurity challenges.

Chapter 13: Third-Party Risk Management

13.1 Assessing Third-Party Risks

Identifying strategies for assessing risks associated with third-party vendors and partners is crucial to protecting the integrity of any organization. A thorough risk assessment process begins with understanding the specific nature of relationships with these third parties. This means evaluating the services they provide and the data they access. Organizations should implement a comprehensive risk management framework that encompasses due diligence processes before entering into partnerships. This involves gathering information on potential vendors' business practices, financial stability, and overall reputation in the marketplace. Continual monitoring must also be a core component of the strategy. Regular checks using automated tools and manual audits can help identify any shifts in a vendor's stability or security posture. Communication is key; establishing clear channels for dialogue with vendors enhances the ability to address potential risks promptly. Integrating a risk-based approach ensures that assessments are tailored to the level of risk each vendor presents, allowing for focused resource allocation towards managing higher-risk partnerships.

Examining frameworks for evaluating third-party security practices is essential to ensure alignment with internal security standards. Various established frameworks, such as NIST Cybersecurity Framework or CIS Controls, provide valuable guidelines to assess a vendor's security posture effectively. Implementing a standardized evaluation checklist based on these frameworks allows organizations to systematically scrutinize how third parties handle sensitive data and infrastructure. This checklist should include aspects such as data encryption practices, incident response protocols, access control measures, and compliance with relevant regulations. Performing gap analyses against these established standards can reveal vulnerabilities and help organizations understand where third-party security practices may not align with their own. Engaging in collaborative risk assessments with third parties can promote transparency and inform both parties of shared risks, leading to better risk remediation strategies. Documenting these evaluations provides a clear audit trail, which can be vital for regulatory compliance and organizational accountability.

Pursuing continuous improvement in the third-party risk assessment process can significantly bolster an organization's resilience. Organizations can consider adopting technologies such as machine learning to enhance their risk identification and management capabilities. These technologies can analyze large volumes of data from various sources to quickly identify potential threats related to third-party relationships. Additionally, fostering a culture of security awareness across all levels of the organization enables teams to recognize the importance of vendor security and actively engage in risk management practices. Training employees on how to report suspicious activities related to third-party partnerships can create a proactive stance against vulnerabilities. Lastly, ensure that there is a clear incident response plan that includes third-party engagements, which guarantees a coordinated effort in the event of a security breach. By prioritizing the assessment and management of third-party risks, organizations can safeguard their networks and maintain trust with their clients and stakeholders.

13.2 Monitoring Third-Party Security Practices

Continuously monitoring third-party security measures is crucial for organizations striving to maintain a robust security posture. The risk landscape often shifts, influenced by various factors such as new vulnerabilities, changes in business operations, or even incidents affecting other clients of a vendor. Best practices for ongoing monitoring include the establishment of clearly defined metrics and benchmarks for evaluating third-party security performance. Regularly reviewing these metrics through audits and assessments helps to identify any deviations from the expected security standards. Additionally, maintaining open lines of communication with third-party vendors fosters a collaborative environment where security concerns can be promptly addressed. Organizations should also consider conducting periodic risk assessments to gauge how shifts in the external landscape, such as regulatory changes or emerging threats, could impact the security of their supply chain. By integrating continuous monitoring into their risk management framework, companies not only detect increased risk levels but are also better prepared to respond effectively.

Technology plays a vital role in enhancing the monitoring of third-party risk and compliance. Advanced tools such as automated vulnerability scanners, security information and event management (SIEM) systems, and cloud-based risk management platforms provide organizations with real-time insights into their vendors' security postures. These technologies enable the collection and analysis of data related to various security events, offering a comprehensive view of third-party activities. Automation can streamline the process of maintaining compliance by continually verifying that vendors adhere to security policies and standards. Furthermore, utilizing machine learning algorithms can help identify patterns or anomalies that may point to potential security issues. By leveraging technology, organizations enhance their ability to monitor and manage the risks associated with third-party vendors effectively, facilitating a proactive approach to security that aligns with their overall risk management strategy.

Incorporating these practices not only mitigates risks but also strengthens the overall resilience of the networks involved. Cyber security professionals should consider implementing a layered approach to third-party risk management that combines human oversight with technological advancements. This approach can lead to more informed decision-making while ensuring that the dynamic nature of third-party security is adequately addressed.

13.3 Integrating Third-Party Assurance into Cyber Resilience

Integrating third-party assurance mechanisms into the broader cyber resilience strategy is essential for organizations aiming to bolster their defenses against cyber threats. As businesses increasingly rely on external vendors and partners for various services, understanding the security postures of these third parties becomes critical. Organizations must evaluate the security controls in place within their suppliers, ensuring they are aligned with their own cybersecurity policies. This can be achieved through comprehensive assessments, contractual agreements that mandate security controls, and ongoing monitoring of third-party compliance. Engaging in regular risk assessments that include third-party vendors helps organizations identify weaknesses and address potential vulnerabilities before they can be exploited. Furthermore, implementing a framework that allows for continuous vetting and management of third-party risks will enable businesses to maintain ongoing cybersecurity resilience.

Examining real-world case studies can shed light on successful approaches to securing third-party relationships. For instance, a leading financial institution implemented a multi-tiered supplier assurance program that involved thorough pre-agreement vetting of security practices, along with regular audits post-contract. This led to a noticeable decrease in security incidents associated with third-party vendors. Another compelling example comes from a healthcare provider that faced significant threats from its data-sharing partnerships. By deploying a system that required all partners to achieve specific cybersecurity certifications and regularly report their security metrics, the provider not only enhanced its security posture but also improved its overall response capabilities during a breach incident. Such examples illustrate the importance of collaboration with third parties to ensure comprehensive security, demonstrating that proactive and structured engagement can yield tangible benefits in cyber resilience.

It's worth noting that integrating third-party assurance is not a one-off effort, but rather a continuous process that evolves alongside changes in technology and the threat landscape. Effective communication and collaboration with third-party partners can pave the way for a robust cyber resilience strategy. Encouraging open dialogue about vulnerabilities, sharing best practices, and fostering a culture of cybersecurity awareness among all stakeholders will significantly strengthen an organization's defenses. A practical tip for cybersecurity professionals is to develop a checklist of key security requirements for third-party vendors, which should be reviewed and updated regularly to ensure relevance in the face of emerging threats. This disciplined approach not only enhances security but also builds a framework of trust and accountability between organizations and their suppliers.

Chapter 14: Cyber Resilience Frameworks and Standards

14.1 Overview of Leading Cyber Resilience Frameworks

Leading frameworks and standards such as the National Institute of Standards and Technology (NIST) Cybersecurity Framework and the International Organization for Standardization (ISO) standards have become critical tools for organizations striving to improve their cyber resilience. The NIST Cybersecurity Framework aids in aligning cybersecurity processes with business objectives, providing a risk-based approach that emphasizes the importance of identifying, protecting, detecting, responding to, and recovering from cyber incidents. Similarly, the ISO standards, particularly ISO/IEC 27001, offer a comprehensive set of guidelines for establishing, implementing, maintaining, and continuously improving an information security management system. These frameworks not only help organizations assess their current cybersecurity posture but also serve as blueprints for developing robust strategies tailored to their unique environments.

While adopting frameworks like NIST and ISO can provide significant benefits, organizations must evaluate these frameworks against their own unique needs and capabilities. The context in which an organization operates—including its size, industry, regulatory requirements, and existing security posture—greatly influences the effectiveness of a chosen framework. For instance, a small healthcare provider may need to prioritize patient data privacy and compliance with HIPAA standards, while a large financial institution may focus more on robust incident response measures and data integrity. This evaluation process involves carefully assessing not only the technical requirements and resources available but also the organizational culture and risk appetite. Organizations should engage relevant stakeholders across the business to understand their specific needs, thereby ensuring the framework selected is not only practical but also enhances overall cyber resilience.

Ultimately, the successful implementation of these frameworks hinges on continuous learning and adaptation. Cyber threats are ever-evolving, necessitating that organizations remain vigilant and proactive in their resilience efforts. Regularly reviewing and refining the chosen framework to suit changing needs is essential. A good practice is to incorporate lessons learned from past incidents and industry developments into the framework to enhance its relevance and effectiveness. This proactive approach not only strengthens the organization's defense but also fosters a culture of resilience that can permeate all levels of the organization.

14.2 Choosing the Right Framework for Your Organization

When selecting a cyber resilience framework, organizations should consider several critical factors that can significantly influence their choice and implementation. First, a clear understanding of the organization's risk landscape is essential. This includes identifying potential threats, vulnerabilities, and the unique business environment in which the organization operates. Regulatory requirements are also a significant factor; organizations may be compelled to follow specific frameworks that satisfy legal or compliance needs. Additionally, the existing technology stack must align with the chosen framework, ensuring compatibility and ease of integration. This requires a thorough evaluation of current security posture and available resources, which will ultimately guide decision-makers in selecting the most appropriate framework that not only meets compliance but also strengthens overall security resilience.

Alignment with the organization's culture and operational goals deeply enhances the effectiveness of any cyber resilience framework. A framework that resonates with the organizational ethos fosters a conducive environment where employees are more engaged and motivated to adhere to security practices. Moreover, when a framework supports the operational goals of the organization—such as promoting innovation, enhancing customer trust, or ensuring business continuity—it can lead to greater investment in resilience initiatives. This connection transforms security from a mere compliance checkbox into a strategic enabler of business success. By integrating cyber resilience into the fabric of the organization, leaders can cultivate a proactive security culture where every member of the team recognizes their role in sustaining a robust cybersecurity posture.

Choosing the right framework is not just a technical decision but a strategic one that requires a comprehensive understanding of both the external and internal factors at play. Incorporating stakeholder input during the selection process can provide valuable insights and enhance commitment to the framework's objectives. Regularly revising the framework based on performance assessments and evolving business needs ensures ongoing relevance and effectiveness. Addressing the human element in cyber resilience cannot be overstated; training programs that explain the importance of the chosen framework and encourage a culture of security will fortify the organization's defenses. Ultimately, the aim should be to develop a resilient organization that is not only prepared for today's threats but can also adapt to future challenges.

14.3 Implementation of Cyber Resilience Standards

Implementing cyber resilience standards within organizational processes and policies requires a clear understanding of the specific frameworks and methodologies that best suit an organization's needs. Start with a comprehensive assessment of current policies, practices, and existing vulnerabilities. This assessment can reveal areas that lack resilience and help prioritize the implementation of necessary standards. Following this, engaging key stakeholders from various departments is crucial. Their insights can help shape policies that are not only robust but also practical and relevant. Training sessions should be initiated to elevate the organization's cybersecurity awareness, ensuring that all employees grasp the importance of cyber resilience. This awareness fosters a culture of security that extends beyond the cybersecurity team, integrating into the daily functions and decision-making processes across the board.

A phased implementation strategy is effective because it allows for gradual integration of resilience standards rather than a disruptive overhaul of the existing systems. Organizations can start by piloting the standards in non-critical areas, which helps identify potential challenges without immediate consequences on vital operations. As feedback is gathered from these initial phases, adjustments can be made before a wider rollout. This iterative approach not only enhances the effectiveness of the standards being implemented but also boosts employee buy-in as they can see the positive impacts firsthand. Additionally, it provides a structured method for testing and measuring resilience, allowing for continual refinement over time. By breaking down implementation into manageable steps, organizations can reduce the risk of failure and increase the overall success rate of integrating cyber resilience within their frameworks.

Ultimately, the path to establishing cyber resilience is ongoing, necessitating regular reviews and updates to the implemented standards. Continuous monitoring and feedback loops are essential to adapt to new threats and changes in the technological landscape. Organizations should remain vigilant, staying informed about the latest best practices and advancements in cybersecurity. This proactive approach not only consolidates the foundations of their resilience but also equips them to respond effectively to emerging challenges, reinforcing their defenses in an ever-evolving threat environment. A practical tip is to create a dedicated team responsible for ongoing evaluation and adaptation of the resilience standards, ensuring they remain relevant and effective against new cyber threats.

Chapter 15: Future Directions in Cyber Resilience

15.1 Evolving Cyber Threats and Resilience Tactics

As the digital landscape becomes increasingly complex, evolving cyber threats necessitate adaptive resilience tactics and proactive defense mechanisms. Cyber adversaries continuously refine their strategies, leveraging advanced technologies to exploit vulnerabilities. This dynamic environment demands that cybersecurity professionals approach resilience not as a static goal but as an ongoing process requiring constant vigilance and agility. Organizations must assess their existing security frameworks and shift from traditional reactive measures to proactive strategies designed to anticipate and mitigate risks before they materialize. By embedding resilience into the very architecture of networks and systems, security professionals can ensure that they are not just responding to threats but also fortifying their defenses against future attacks. Factors like supplier assurance and defense in depth play pivotal roles in constructing multi-layered security architectures that are robust, adaptable, and capable of withstanding a variety of threats.

The need for continuous research and innovation in resilience approaches is paramount to combat future threats. As cyber threats evolve, so too must the methodologies employed to counteract them. This includes investing in new technologies, developing machine learning algorithms for threat detection, and exploring collaborative frameworks that enhance information sharing across sectors. Such innovation can significantly improve incident response times and threat mitigation strategies, offering an edge in a landscape characterized by rapid change. Furthermore, engaging with academic institutions, startups, and cross-industry forums can foster an ecosystem of experimentation and knowledge exchange. By prioritizing research and innovation, cybersecurity professionals not only enhance their immediate defense capabilities but also contribute to a broader culture of resilience that can adapt to the uncertainties of tomorrow.

Developing a culture of resilience within organizations also involves ongoing training and education for all personnel. Cybersecurity is not solely the responsibility of the IT department; it requires a holistic approach where every employee understands their role in safeguarding information and infrastructure. By integrating resilience into organizational practices and cultivating a mindset that values cybersecurity as a shared responsibility, organizations can create a united front against evolving cyber threats. This cultural shift, paired with cutting-edge technology and innovative practices, underscores the importance of a proactive stance in cybersecurity that anticipates challenges rather than merely reacting to them.

15.2 Role of Collaboration in Enhancing Resilience

Cross-industry collaboration and information-sharing are pivotal for enhancing collective cyber resilience. As cyber threats evolve, the need for a united front becomes critical. When organizations from different sectors come together, they pool resources, share intelligence, and leverage diverse expertise. This collaboration creates a robust defense mechanism that individual enterprises may struggle to achieve on their own. By openly sharing threat intelligence, organizations can respond more effectively to potential vulnerabilities. Moreover, this exchange fosters a deeper understanding of emerging threats and the development of better strategies to mitigate them. In a landscape where time is of the essence, realizing that collective resilience is more effective than individual efforts can make all the difference in combating cyber threats.

Establishing effective partnerships between organizations is crucial for mutual security advantages. To do this, creating a framework that facilitates communication and collaboration is essential. Organizations should start by identifying common goals and areas where they can mutually benefit. Regular joint exercises and simulations can help build trust and understanding of each other's infrastructures and security postures. Employing structured agreements, such as Information Sharing and Analysis Centers (ISACs), enhances the capacity to share sensitive information while addressing legal and regulatory concerns. These frameworks can also include routine assessments and feedback loops to gauge the effectiveness of the collaboration. The relationship should evolve continuously based on insights gained from shared experiences, fostering a culture where each partner feels empowered to contribute actively to its shared cyber defense.

To truly harness the power of collaboration, organizations should focus on creating an open culture of trust and transparency. This not only involves sharing technical information but also extending to sharing governance practices and incident response strategies. Networking with other professionals in the industry can also reveal valuable lessons and practices that have been effective in other contexts. Implementing regular workshops and forums can facilitate knowledge transfer and strengthen ties between collaborating organizations. As cyber threats continue to grow in complexity, enhancing resilience through collaborative efforts will not only improve the security posture of individual organizations but will also contribute to a more secure digital ecosystem overall.

15.3 Anticipating Future Regulatory Changes

As we delve into the intricacies of regulatory frameworks affecting cyber resilience, it becomes evident that organizations must closely analyze trends to brace themselves for upcoming regulations. The landscape of cyber security regulations is evolving rapidly, influenced by technological advancements, emerging threats, and the growing importance of data protection. Regulating bodies are increasingly focusing on industry standards that emphasize accountability and resilience. For instance, frameworks such as GDPR and CCPA set stringent guidelines for data management and user privacy, prompting organizations to adapt their cyber resilience practices accordingly. By understanding these shifts, cyber security professionals can prepare their organizations for compliance, ensuring they remain agile and responsive to new mandates. Monitoring policy evolutions across various sectors and keeping abreast of leading examples can serve as valuable touchpoints for implementation, as organizations strive not only to comply with current regulations but to lead in industrial best practices.

Proactive strategies play a crucial role in aligning with anticipated regulatory changes and ensuring sustained compliance. Organizations should adopt a forward-thinking mindset by engaging in continuous risk assessments and scenario planning. This allows companies to identify potential gaps in their existing frameworks and address them before regulations are enacted. Creating flexible compliance protocols, which can evolve with changing regulations, will enhance organizational resilience. Training and development programs targeting both technical and managerial staff are essential, fostering a culture of compliance awareness throughout the workforce. Additionally, collaboration with regulatory bodies and industry peers can provide insights into future developments, allowing organizations to stay abreast of potential changes. By fostering strong relationships with regulators and investing in technology to automate compliance processes, companies can streamline adapting to future regulations and maintain robust security postures.

Ultimately, preparing for future regulatory changes is not merely a reactive measure, but an integral part of an organization's culture and operational strategy. Building resilience into the network design ensures that compliance is woven into the very fabric of the organization. Cyber security professionals can utilize frameworks such as supplier assurance and defense in depth, aligning their practices with anticipated regulations. Emphasizing comprehensive documentation, regular audits, and a transparent communication strategy will facilitate smoother transitions as new regulations arise. By taking these steps, organizations not only protect themselves against potential legal repercussions but also fortify their reputations, positioning themselves as trusted entities within the digital economy.

www.ingramcontent.com/pod-product-compliance
Lightning Source LLC
LaVergne TN
LVHW060124070326
832902LV00019B/3134